DO NOT STAND AT MY GRAVE AND WEEP

Anonymous

Designed and illustrated by
Paul Saunders

SOUVENIR PRESS

Do not stand at my grave and weep

I am not there.

I do not sleep.

I am a thousand winds that blow

I am the diamond glints on snow.

I am the sunlight on ripened grain

I am the gentle autumn rain.

When you awaken in the morning's hush,

I am the swift uplifting rush
Of quiet birds

in circled flight.

I am the soft stars that shine at night.

Do not stand at my grave and cry,

I am not there;

I did not die.

The poem printed in this book,
by an unknown author,
was found in an envelope left by a soldier
killed by an exploding mine
near Londonderry in 1989.
It was read aloud by his father
on the BBC Television programme *Bookworm*
on Remembrance Sunday, 1995,
evoking a huge and warm response
from viewers all over the country.

This Edition first published 1996 by
Souvenir Press Ltd,
43 Great Russell Street, London WC1B 3PA

Reprinted 1996, 1997, 1998 (twice), 1999 (twice), 2000

ISBN 0 285 63335 X

Photoset by Rowland Phototypesetting Ltd
Bury St Edmunds, Suffolk
Printed in Italy